Business Plan Pro: The Secrets to Writing A Successful Business Plan That is Guaranteed To Win Investors!

Table of Contents

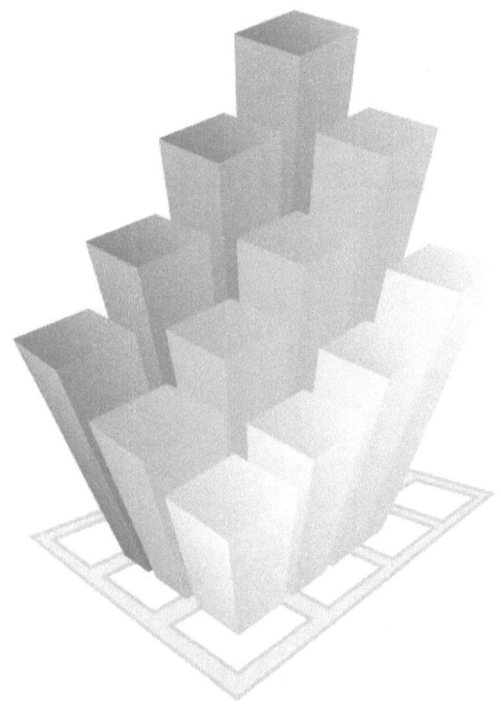

A business plan is one of the most important documents that an entrepreneur or business owner should carefully and painstakingly craft and develop, in order to attract and retain investors. So it's vital that business owners and up-and-coming entrepreneurs have the necessary information and skills needed to understand how to write a business plan that is guaranteed to get investors interested, and retain that interest. Read on to get the skills to perform this important business task.

Introduction

The process of developing and writing a quality, credible business plan shows whether or not a business is potentially profitable. The process of putting statistical figures, facts and other important business functions onto paper ensures that the business has a better chance of attracting investors along with the much needed capital. In this book you'll get a comprehensive insight into the process of how to write a business plan that is practically guaranteed to get your investors knocking at your door.

Business plans can also be used as a marketing or sales tools to attract partners, funding organizations or executive level employees. In all business outfits, a business plan and business planning in general is a very important and necessary activity. This should be done by every business that is focused towards achieving business success in the face of challenging circumstances and competition.

It does not matter whether the business is in the start-up stage or has been operational for a long time. Business planning is crucial, necessary and important in ensuring the success of every business regardless of its stage in the business development cycle. There is therefore a need for every business manager, every business owner or every person over whose shoulders the sole activity of business planning rests, to have the proper and in-depth knowledge on how to write and develop a working business plan that will not only attract investors but also that will ensure the business succeeds to maturity.

The process is not difficult for a motivated entrepreneur, <u>compared to the difficulties that will crop up if the document is not written at all</u>.

It is therefore important for every business owner to have the basics of do-it-yourself when it comes to proper business planning.

There is every reason why all business operations should have a clear and concise business focus. It is a common misconception among many entrepreneurs that business plans are synonymous with businesses that are just starting up. Many misinformed business owners and managers think that business plans are only supposed to be drafted and written by those business that are rolling out for the first time or those ones that are struggling to get on their feet. There is nothing that could be further from the truth.

Business plans are supposed to be written, and sometimes re-written, adjusted and re-adjusted by both startups, operating and mature businesses. Planning is one of the best things that a business can do whether the entity is a multinational, regional, national, a proprietorship, or just a startup. Even when a multinational company is trying to extend and spread its wings to cover more areas and operational branches, planning is one of most crucial thing that the business managers should be thinking about. This applies to even small startups that also need to plan and succeed in business. It is needless to mention also that even the slightest business idea can be actualized by the use of a proper and well-thought out business plan.

Despite the fact that many business owners and managers think that business plans are meant for the small startups and small companies, the entrepreneurs on the other end tend to think that business plans are only meant for the "big" companies that have millions of dollars in turnover, multiple business products, thousands of employees and a million other business related issues. This is the reason why many business owners that run "small" companies and those ones that are just rolling out do not actually spend a lot of time in business planning. Another reason behind this misconception is the fact that these business operators are not aware of how easy it can be making, drafting and writing a business plan that will attract investors from every corner.

Most small business owners and operators are scared stiff when they hear such professional terms as used in business such as strategic planning, tactical planning and so forth. They usually cower and scamper to the "safety" of ignorance rather than spending a little time to capture, understand and internalize these terms that will determine the success or failure of their businesses and business operations. Grasping the basics of business planning and writing a business plan is one of the most fundamental issues that determine the success or failure of the business.

Small business owners and some companies tend to disregard business planning…at their own peril. Business planning is usually a time-consuming activity and often happens when the business is not earning anything. So small business owners and operators tend to disregard business planning due to the fact that this coincides with when they are earning the least or earning nothing at all. Instead of engaging business planning, they first engage the one that they think will bring in profits faster, only to realize that they made the biggest of mistakes. In this way, drafting a good and credible business plan, though time-consuming, outweighs the risks of losing your investments later due to poor planning.

It can be fairly easy to start up a business project but without proper plan, it is like going to a distant place without a roadmap. Even though you can still end up reaching your destination without the roadmap, it will be astonishing looking back and getting to understand the many times that you get lost along the way and the amount of time and resources you spent trying to blindly reach your destination. So which is better, to wander in the desert without a compass or to drive straight to your destination using the best of geo-positioning technology? Writing a credible business plan is the key to any business venture.

Writing a working and credible business plan is the key to getting investors, partners, donors, funds and becoming successful in the business venture in question. It is therefore very important to get the best way through which one can write a credible business plan that will attract and retain investors, customers, and all those players that matter most in the business venture. In this book, we are going to learn how to write a business plan that is guaranteed to get your investors interested and running towards your business.

What Is a Business Plan?

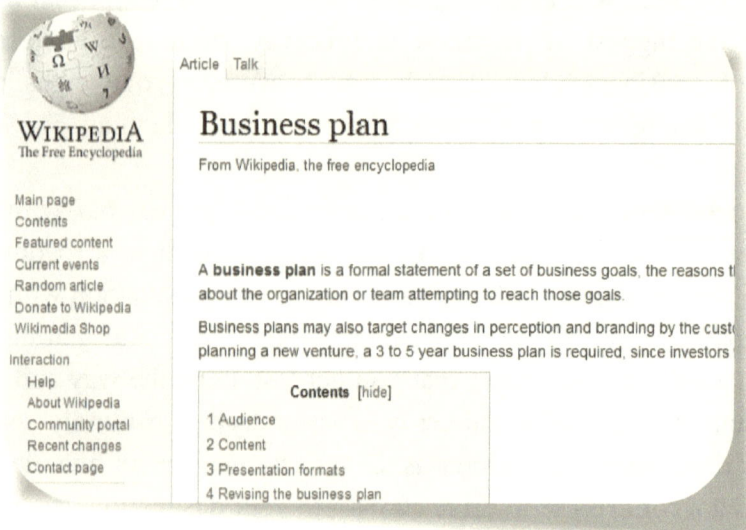

The dictionary will tell you that a business, in relation to what we are discussing here, "is the activity of providing goods and services to consumers...." And that the activity of doing this has a commercial or industrial element attached to it. Once you are deep into the academics of these issues where you will start hearing such jargon as finance, marketing, profit margins, turnovers, balance sheets....many business operators just shy off and lock out what would have otherwise benefited not only their knowledge base but their business ventures. In as much as the business element can be innately embedded on the business owner's self, the process of learning a few things here and there, especially the process of writing a good and credible business plan can be very beneficial and important in the overall business performance.

By the same token, a plan is a series of actions or steps to be taken or carried out, or goals or objectives to be carried out. Others can see it as a scheme of things or a schedule to be followed. Architects will want to see the plan as a "scale drawing" without which the building cannot be built. This is not an inch different from what the plan is supposed to be in business. This does not matter whether the plan is in your head or you have carefully and painstakingly put it on paper. The purpose of this book is to show you how you should carefully and professionally put your business plan on paper in the most expertly manner.

So what is a business plan? According to WordWeb, a popular online dictionary, a business plans is "A summary of how a business owner, manager, or entrepreneur intends to organize an entrepreneurial endeavor and implement activities for the venture to succeed" This means that a business plan is a representation of what the business owner intends to do for his business operation to succeed. By the term summary, a business plan therefore entails all that there is in the business from the onset to maturity and beyond.

And according to WikiPedia.org, a business plan is "a formal statement of a set of business goals, the reasons they are believed attainable, and the plan for reaching those goals. It may also contain background information about the organization or team attempting to reach those goals."

In a professional sense, a business plan is a document that lays out all the specific details of your business. This does not matter whether the document is a few sentences, pages or volumes in size. In fact, business plans range from a few sentences to the most voluminous depending on the type of business. However, special caution and professionalism should be applied when writing a credible business plan even when it comes to the size of the document as we shall see later in this book.

A business plan is therefore a future-focused professional description of how you intend to operate as a <u>commercially and financially viable entity</u>.

he plan includes all what you intend to do so that your business can become successful. Every business has a particular and different plan depending on its operations but essentially, there is that standard business plan that all businesses should conform to. This book will discuss in details all what a good and credible business plan should entail.

In communications circles, a good and credible business plan should conform to the basic four "W"s and one "H" (who, when, what, where and how). This means that a good and credible business plan should tell who is involved in the business, when the business will operate, commence or last; what the business entails where and how it will operate. In addition to these basics, a credible and professional business plan will tell providing reasons why particular decisions have been made and why leave the others. In this way, there will be a proper justifications and background evidence.

A business plan therefore entails all those activities intended to be performed or provided so that a particular firm realizes success in both its operations and profitability. These activities may collectively be referred to as business planning activities. According to Rodney Jones, an Associate Professor / Extension Livestock Production Economics at Kansas State University, business planning "is all about finding, describing, and refining the competitive advantage of a particular firm or entity to assist that firm in achieving individual goals and objectives (financial, transitional, resource stewardship, family, etc.).”

In this way, business planning is <u>not a once-off activity</u> but a process that recurs to ensure that the business succeeds in every stage of development.

It is a notable fact that business planning happens amid other defining and affecting issues such as the particular goals and objectives of the business. In addition to this, most business managers will agree to the fact that planning is a valuable aspect of business success but the time cost remains the stumbling block towards this initiative. In this way, despite the fact that the business managers will realize the importance of business plan, they may remain adamant due to the time cost involved.

This book will outline the importance of spending time on writing a winning and a credible business plan that will give the business a cutting edge in getting investors. According to Jones, there is always a need to ensure that business owners and operators conform to a set of planning code that will lead to success of the business. This includes clear goals and objectives. He asserts that “among other characteristics, businesses that succeed tend to have realistic expectations and a clear sense of purpose (they stick to a well-defined set of core values). Successful businesses monitor costs and profitability, and they develop an understanding of their strengths and weaknesses.” There is therefore a need for you as an entrepreneur to have the skills required to develop a working business plan.

All this serves to show the business owner or operator the importance of spending time in writing a credible business plan. Investing time and other resources in developing a credible and professional business plan is the most valuable activity that a business owner or operator should undertake and do it well.

Writing a good, credible and professional business plan is the first essential aspect of ensuring that your business succeeds. This will provide you with a roadmap, a good direction for business success. In addition to providing you with the business future, a credible a well-written business plan is essential towards attracting funding and donors.

Why Is A Business Plan Essential in Business Operations?

According to David Bryson, most entrepreneurs start with the deck stacked against them. Schools taught them only to be employees. With an idea in hand, they start out lacking even basic knowledge of how to run a business. There is therefore a need to learn how to plan and execute business ideas and activities. There are many reasons why a business plan is essential for business. Among the most important of these reasons include the following;

- **It is essential in managing your business operations such as finances.**

- It is useful when it comes to laying out strategic actions towards business development.

- **The business owner will be able to focus on the business activities without too much worry, as everything is captured in the plan.**

- The owner or operator of the business will be able to measure the business success against projected lines.

- **The business will operate in an organized manner instead of the haphazard decisions made without proper planning.**

- Provides the best ways through which the business owner or operator can do research and collect important data concerning the industry that the business lies.

- **The collected information concerning the business will mean that the owner of the business is given a winning edge in the face of stiff competition and changing business circumstances.**

- A business plan is essential in the sense that it is a clear representation of the business operations intended and done. It will also provide projections for the future and makes it possible for the business future to be taken into account and planned for.

- **A business plan is a serious business document that represents all that there is in the business. In this sense,** it is essential that the business manager prevents it from falling in the wrong hands such as those of the competitor. Your business plan is an important document that should be filed and archived safely.

The Importance of a Business Plan

There is every reason why businesses regardless of their size should be sure to write and update a strategic and accurate business plan. In this way, the business owner or manager should clearly know the importance of writing a good and credible business plan. It is important to note that a business plan is a document that is highly predictive, more so when the business is only in its startup stage. So it follows that the planner should be sure that the predictions are accurate and plausible in the context of the business in question. The assumptions made should be convincing enough to the reader such that the assumptions will serve to persuade the reader that whatever is being predicted is credible and conceivable in the totality and contextual business circumstances.

Once the business is up and operating, the business plan will have a historical point of reference where the planner can look at and provide suitable and accurate forecasts in relation to the business and assumptions thereof. In as much as the plan should be certain and reflect proper assumption, it is true that we are faced with lots of uncertainties day in day out. We are always being faced with situations that are uncertain and therefore require proper intervention. This is the main reason why every business should operate and write a credible business plan to cater for these uncertainties.

Every business owner or manager is continually confronted by strategic and tactical business issues in the process of business operations. Having a credible business plan will give the owner or manager a way out of this problems, giving him a perfect chance to focus on the business issues rather than responding to haphazard business circumstances. Among the most important reasons why a business plan is important includes the following;

a) Provide a business focus to both the manager and the employees of the firm. This means that the plan will calculate the best way through which the business should move on. Instead of the employees and managers relying on haphazard emails, phone calls, texts and so on, the business will assume a proactive dimension that will guide it through to success. Instead of waiting for these important communications from your customers or clients, the business plan will provide a special focus that will lead the business towards proactively consulting, contacting and reaching out to the clients, customers, business partners and investors depending on the prevailing angle you are considering for your business.

b) In the process of putting your business idea, thoughts, actions and activities on paper, you will get a perfect chance to understand your business better and map out a specific business course. In so doing, the manager will get to the details of these business courses of actions and project their best possible times to initialize and execute. In relation to this, the planner will have the chance to chart out other possible alternatives to particular business actions current or future. This is without mentioning that the planner will also set very clear goals and objectives touching on the business area. There is nothing more important than setting crystal clear business goals and objectives, no matter what the situation.

c) The business plan will allow the planner to touch on the business resources and budget. There is nothing more important than having a clear look at the business resources and where these will come from. This will help the business to deal with one of the most important business areas that touch on budgeting and funding. Once you set the goals and objectives of your business, you will want to know where the resources to actualize these goals and objectives will come from.

d) A good and credible business plan will allow you to manage a quality cash flow system. In the case of reduced sales volumes, a good plan will allow you to project and manage alternative actions that will serve as a remedy to reduced sales. In this way, you will have formulated a system that will allow the business to thrive amidst reduced or decreasing sales volumes. There is no way that you will maneuver from this scenario if your business does not have a concrete and concise plan.

e) In many cases, you will find your business in need of proper credit management system. Some creditors and debtors will run out of business while you still need to recover the debts as well as pay your creditors. A proper plan will allow you to get to the roots of credit and debt management where you will have laid in place alternative payment methods. A proper plan will allow you to get to the roots of your credit control systems, the invoicing and banking facilities to ensure that you are on top of your business control systems at all times, no matter what.

f) The other importance of a good plan is that it will help you to do a proper business performance assessment. Remember that the plan is futuristic approach to your business operations. In this way, you will have the chance to look at actual business performance vis a vis projected or intended performance. This will help you gauge the performance of your business and see whether you are on the right track. Once you realize that the business has derailed from the projected path, you can implement remedial measures that will ensure that you are on the right track. Once you see that your business is performing to the projected expectations, you can be sure to do even better by implementing commensurate measures to ensure that you proceed that way or even better. The plan can also give out responsibilities to particular individuals in business and you as the manager.

g) A business plan is a crucial tool in the management of the overall issues touching on the business idea. From employee management and product and services management to risk and insurance, a good business plan is holistic and all-inclusive. The document will provide a relevant roadmap, direction and references for all business operations throughout the life of the enterprise.

h) A business plan is essential in the process of securing funding such as from banks and other financial institutions. Every business needs both startup and operating capital. There is no way you can be certain of getting loans and other financial aid from well-established financial institutions without first creating a well written business plan. An operating business will also need additional funding for buying property and products such as business equipment. Writing a proper plan will give as an entrepreneur a perfect chance to attract and secure funding from established financial institutions for much needed operational and expansion funds.

i) As a management tool, a business plan is essential in making competent management possible. Good planners understand that businesses are dynamic and change over time as more goals and objectives crop up in the process of operating the business. The original business plan changes over time as new channels and goals crop up and need to be factored in to business operations. In this way, a plan will tell you the best ways of doing this, the areas that need assessment and adjustment and the areas that will need to be improved upon.

j) Among the most important reasons for writing a viable plan for your business, and which of course is the original aspect of this book, is to attract investors. In the process of looking for venture capitalist or even angel investors for your business, you will need a proper, credible and solid business plan. Even after doing a credible business presentation to your potential investors that may attract their attention, they will need a proper document that they will want to study before making any meaningful investment commitment to your business or organization.

Your plan must be well scrutinized by venture capitalist or angel investors and background checks done before they actually commit to investment. In this sense you will need to have this in mind and develop a winning plan for your investors. They will also need to perform a competitive analysis and get to see whether what you have laid down is actually the case before they engage the necessary investment commitment. In this way, you will need to have the necessary information on how to write a plan document that will not only attract the investors but also retain them for business purposes.

The Writing Process

Before writing your business plan, it is very much important to understand the most common mistakes that entrepreneurs and small business owners and managers make in the process. Among the most common mistakes in the writing process include the following;

a) **Mistake #1:** Failing to write a business plan in the first place! This is the most common mistake that entrepreneurs and business owners make. Failing to make a good business plan document is the most common and sure way of business failures across all levels of business cycle and maturity. Every business person or lay person in any trade has heard of the axiom that "he who fails to plan…plans to fail". This means that if you fall short of planning, you have contributed towards your own failure. This is the most certain path that a business will follow in the process of planning failure. This only serves to remind business owners and managers that a business plan is the most important aspect of any enterprise.

b) **Mistake #2:** Not being 100% clear in your mind about the purpose of your business outline. It is important to note that a business outline or plan document is a solution to a problem rather than just another business document. The document serves to solve the problem of how you will need to conduct your business in the surest way towards success. In this way, the document will serve to tell you as an entrepreneur how you are going to transform your business idea to real business profits and success. So, the business plan should be very clear in mind on the purpose of making the business plan in the first place. Are you looking for a chance to write a persuasive document for your business to attract funds and loans from lenders, donors, etc? Are you looking for investors and business success? In this way, you will have made the first step towards success if you are clear in your mind about what your comprehensive business plan needs to capture.

c) **Mistake #3:** Failing to implement an excellent business model. This is another very common mistake that entrepreneurs and business planners fail to realize. A good business model is very important and should be captured in the business plan. A business model is not haphazard and should be well thought out and applied. In this sense, merely planning to sell something is not a good business model on its own. A good business model in this regard is selling that thing over and above the expenses incurred in the process. It is a plan that aims at generating revenue in the process of doing business.

d) In this way, you can manufacture the best and most comfortable car in the world that will cost you say $50,000 but most people interested in that vehicle may only be willing to pay $20,000 for the car. A good business model will capture that and serve to tell you that you need not engage in such a business. Though you are making and selling the item with a price tag, customers are not willing to buy the item in the tag that you have put. It is therefore not worth pursuing. Going down that path can only be explained by the fact that you are looking for personal satisfaction rather than business ideals. Make a good business plan that will allow the business to generate revenue rather than serve the interests of the heart. There is no point of being labeled the best manufacturer, yet running the business at a loss. Make sure people want to buy what you sell.

e) **Mistake #4:** Failing to conduct proper and in-depth research before writing the business plan. This is another very common mistake that is done by entrepreneurs and business owners. It is important to note that your plan will only be as good and as practical as the research you do prior to writing it. It has been said once and again that when you want to capture the best out of anything, understand it first. In this way, you may want to visualize this as the process of planning how to plan. In the process of gauging whether the business will work, you will need to be familiar with all the aspects that will affect your business in the long run. This is of very high importance to your plan.

f) Among the most common aspects that you should be conversant with are the trends in your market segment. You also need to look and understand your competitors and the strategies towards outdoing them. Though every business is unique, you need to gather as much information as possible before writing and implementing your business plan. This will tell you whether the plan will work or whether you need to shelve the idea and move to another one. Fortunately, a lot of research can be done online and that there is a lot of information in this area. What you need is the willingness to do it and of course the time investment.

g) **Mistake #5:** Failing to conduct good market analysis. Many business managers are quick at ignoring a very important business aspect when writing down their business plan. Market realities are one of the most important aspects that should be considered when writing a business plan. There are three things that serve to describe a good business; there is you and what you want to do, the third is the market of your product or service.

h) Having the best product in the market is just one thing, finding customers interested in the product is another thing that is somewhat independent of the fact that the product is good. If no one is interested in the product, there is no need of availing it in the market in the first place. In this way, you should test the market and see whether your product will sell before actually engaging in the business. There is no point of planning how to sell a product that will not be of interest to any customers in the market. You can start by testing your product locally or online before actually basing a business on the product.

i) **Mistake #6:** Ignoring other indirect competitors in the industry. Among the most common mistakes made by business planners is ignoring the fact that there myriads of competitors that may seem distant but also very vital in the business competition arena. There are those competitors that are not in the same region as your business such as those in distant places and others online. For example, if you are planning to sell groceries, you may fail to factor in the fact that there are other grocers in distant towns and other that sell the same commodities online. How are you going to deal with this in addition to the ones that are in the same locality as your business? A good business plan will outline how you are going to deal with the totality of competition rather than just one segment. Though you may not have to list all competitors, it is important to outline how you will deal with the competition.

j) **Mistake #7:** Failing to perform deep financial analysis. Another very important thing that you need to do as a business planner is to ensure that you have figured out how your business will perform in terms of finances. Many business planners fail to capture this and end up doing badly in business. Among the most important financial documents that should be of importance in creating a good business plan include the balance sheet, the cash flow projection and the income statement. There is no way that you will develop and come up with a good plan if you are not sure the amount of money that your business will need when starting up or operating. Think about and understand the expenses that your business operations will incur and see whether that is operational when it comes to generating revenue. Many planners omit this section or underestimate the expenses that the business will incur. There is every need to do a proper and thorough research into whatever expenses your business will attract. Another important issue to avoid being too optimistic on your business prospects. You should understand that your business operations will be independent of your optimism and that it will happen amid real business environment that does not really care about your thoughts, only business reality.

k) **Mistake #8:** After writing a good and working business plan, many planners make the mistake of putting it aside and operating as if they never wrote the plan in the first place. As an entrepreneur, you need to write the plan and <u>stick to it</u>. You need to have it serve as reference point as well as a roadmap towards your business plan. There is no point of writing a good business plan for the sake of it. Even if you secure the funds and the investors, you still need to have your plan used and executed in totality. Always consult your plan and make additions to it. Have your mission statements properly added as re-adjusted to suit changing business circumstances as they arise in your industry.

l) **Mistake #9:** Failing to <u>know when to quit</u>. It is important to realize that you do not need to continue on a plan to its end. This means that the answer to whether your business idea will work or fail does not emerge at the end; it comes to the fore in the process of implementation. In this way, if the plan is not working, you may need to cut it off or shelve it and move on with another plan. This literally takes into account the fact that you will have no business obligation to finish that business plan that is not working in the first place.

m) **Mistake #10:** Failing to share their business initiatives and plans with people that matter in the process of doing business. Your business life is not independent of other aspects of social life. You should therefore share the plans with your spouse, family and other significant people that will be affected in the process of doing business. This is for example when you are doing business trips, when answering calls, attending to the various issues.

n) **Mistake #11:** Failing to share the business plans with management team, other employees and new hires. In this way, the plan should be part of employee training tools.

Business Plan Writing Steps

Before writing your business plan, you should get clear on issues that will affect the business. You need to do proper and honest evaluation and see whether you business idea will work or whether you desired business needs will finally bear fruits. In this way, you should do the following;

a) Have a deep look at your business idea and ascertain its feasibility. Evaluate whether your business idea can work and whether it is profitable to go down that path. Get as much information as possible about your market and competitors. Researching on the aspect that will affect your business is important as it will help you answer some of the most important question fact come to play in the success of your business idea. Among the most important question that you should seek answers for include the following components;

- ***What product or service provision will I engage in?*** Different product and services have different circumstances when it comes to marketing and competition. Getting at the roots of your products and services will tell you the type of strategies that you need to implement when making your business plan.

- ***Is my business idea feasible?*** There is no point of making a plan on a business plan that is not viable in the first place. Make sure to evaluate your business plan on viability and practicability.

- ***What the steps and resources at my disposal that will allow me to secure and protect my business idea and plan?*** There are several ways that you can protect your intellectual and copyright issues. In this way, you need to evaluate whether you need to invoke legal steps upon having your intellectual rights safeguarded.

- You also need to evaluate ***whether your business products and services have market potential*** by conducting a proper market research and analysis. You need to have your ideal business product having a sure market segment that will generate sufficient revenue and make your business a successful one.

- Evaluate ***whether you have the expertise, the skills and prowess*** needed by your business idea. Be sure to evaluate whether your employees have that or whether you need to have training sessions whether formal or informal. Remember that if you need business training or any of your employees will need one, you will have to factor that in to your business plan in the area of expenses.

- Evaluate *whether you have the finances required* or whether you need to factor that when you are writing the business plan.

b) Self-analysis is also very important in business. You need to have specific and honest answers to whether you are suited as a person to start or mange the type of business that you have in mind. You need to be sure that you have the capacity to maintain and sustain the business amidst other intervening individual and personal decisions and obligations. In this way, you need specific and honest answers to the following important questions;

- *What are the reasons of my staring this business?* Can you get specific reasons why you are starting this business? There arc many reasons why you can start a business but the most vital of all of them is to generate revenue. There are many ways through which you can generate revenue, but why have you chosen this particular business idea for your cash flow and revenue generation?

- *What are the specific personal and business goals in this venture?* Are there some special and personal goals that have the potential of interfering with the overall business operations? How will I manage this in my organization?

- ***What are the skills needed for this business venture?*** Do I or my employees have these skills? If the answer is no, what are measures to be taken?

- ***What are some of the expected obstacles towards achieving these business goals and objectives?*** Are there strategic measures in place to handle these obstacles?

c) Implement strategies aimed at having a proper education in the business area of your choice. The process of looking for the proper information concerning an industry that you are interested in is not only simple but accessible by many. These education chances can be sourced locally or remotely. They include attending seminars, trade shows, symposiums, business meetings, and other business events. Here you can get information that touches on issues like business planning; management of finances, marketing management and other important areas that will leave you well informed.

d) Consider whether you need a business coach, mentor or business incubation service. These are important in the sense that you will get instructions on how you can become successful in your business. Business incubation services may be given for free by government agencies or by a few private enterprises. Consider whether you need these extra outside services and plan for them in your business outline.

e) Remember to write a catchy executive summary of your plan document. This summary should appear first in your plan document but should be written last. It will capture the gist of the plan in a brief and concise manner. This is the first thing that your investors will be looking at when they read your document. In this way, the section should be written last but should include all you want to tell your investors in a summary way.

f) Include a description of the industry that your business wants to venture into. Remember that this is the industry that your business will be part of and that you should show how the business will fit in, describe the major industry players in this section and provide a description of the main industry trends. Give estimates of the industry statistical figures in terms of sales being as most accurate as possible. You should be sure to show the investors your position in this industry and give proper estimates if your business is a startup.

g) Do a proper market analysis. What is your primary target market for your products and/or services? What geographical areas are you intending to target for your products? What are the demographics of the market? What are the market needs and how are they being met in the current time? Remember that this should be done in a descriptive manner and that it should capture the reality on the ground. Give proper estimates in case your business is a startup and provide as accurate and realistic a scenario as possible.

h) Provide a competitive analysis of your business competitors both direct and indirect. Tell the investors who are these and how you will overcome this competition. What is your competitive edge and how are you going to manage any obstacles into this competition? You should be very clear and focused on this so much so that you will need to convince the investor to commit to your needs after reading your business plan.

i) Marketing plans should also be included in this document to show the investor your sales strategy, pricing, advertising and promotion plans for your goods and/or services. Be as detailed as possible and provide the investor with proper and convincing strategic projections on how your marketing plan will benefit the business.

j) Another important thing that you can do is to provide the investor with a working management plan detailing your human resources, internal and external management teams as well as your business legal structures and resources. This will serve to give the investor an insight into the external and internal resources at your disposal and how you plan to benefit your business using the resources provided.

k) There is no way your business will perform well without a proper operating structure. In this way, you will need to provide the investor with a proper business operating plan. This will capture your operating locations, supplies and manufacturers depending on the type of business that you are planning to operate. If you are already in the market, you will need to provide these details in the most accurate manner. If you are just starting up, you will need to provide estimates and plans on your inventory needs, operating plans and the process through which you will acquire or manufacture the sales products.

l) The most important reason for providing a business plan to investors is to secure funding. In this way, there is no point of writing the plan if you will not give your investors a chance to scrutinize you financials in the finance plan section. You will need to furnish your investors with a proper financial plan that captures your funding requirements. In this way, you will also provide them with actual or estimated financial statements and proper analysis of the same. This will depend on whether you are starting up or you are already in business. This will serve to show your investors your financial situation and your plan's viability.

m) A good business plan document usually relies on other supporting documents. These documents should be listed in appended to the final plan document. You will also want to include other supporting documents that will serve to increase the credibility of your plan document. These documents may be such as photos of your products, legal contractual documents, marketing study documents as well as any other document that you think will be of use in the investment-seeking process.

Sections of a Business Plan

It imperative for all entrepreneurs and business managers to understand that a good business plan should be clear, concise and structured in order to capture all the needed issues. In this way, depending on the type of business in question, structured document sections as included in this list. Among the most prominent sections that should not be forgotten include the following;

a) **The title page**. This section deals with what the plan is all about. It will serve to describe all what the business plan is for and give general information on the business idea. It is important to draft a good and accurate document title that will ensure that investors and other stakeholders are persuaded to look at the contents of your business plan. Remember to include all the details that are consistent with your plan.

b) **About business section**. This is the section that deals with the totality of the business from its products and services, management issues, business ownership, business structure, all management and operational issues. This is popularly referred to as the management or operation plan. This should be properly addressed as it is the gist behind business plan in the first place. This is the section that is the body of the plan and should be carefully and exhaustively written. Some refer to this as the business details section that outlines the business operations as they are or as they are intended to be.

c) **Business registration section**. This section deals with the official registration details of your business. This should focus on what is included in your business official registration documents and certificates. The information inserted here should be accurate and verifiable for the sake of increasing the credibility of your plan document. You should also remember to attach these documents when you finish writing your plan.

d) **Business location section**. This is the section where you will enter the premises of your business. Many credible planners usually provide a map that will tell the investor where the business is located. In these recent times where businesses are purely online or virtual in operation, you should indicate this and provide the relevant details of your virtual offices. These may be websites, mobile resources, web tools or cloud services.

e) **Business summary**. This should be written after everything has been done in terms of writing the document. In this sense, the summary should capture all what the business plan is all about in a concise and professional manner. Although this section is written last, it should appear first in your plan document, to summarize the plan.

f) **Market section**. This will serve to show your marketing requirements, expectations and strategies. You can provide your marketing analysis and issues concerning the industry that you are venturing into, provide an analysis of your competitors and how you plan to overcome the products and services that your industry competitors are providing.

g) **Financial section**. This deals with what your business finances will look like and how you plan to source them. In this way, you will provide the necessary information that touches on the finances and how you plan to invest funds as you start and grow the business.

h) **Innovation section**. This will deal with the part of your business that is unique and provides a cutting edge benefit in your business. You will need to show the investor how creative you are in business and how this will help your business to grow to maturity most profitably.

i) **Risk management and insurance section**. This is the section that will tell the investor how you will deal with business risks and the amount and type of insurance that your business will acquire or has already acquired. This is important in the sense that the investor will be put in the know about the preparations and structures put in place by the planner in relation to business risks and how to tackle them effectively.

j) **Legal section**. This will inform the investor on the legal issues that the business may encounter. In this way, the planner will provide the necessary legal documents that the business will be using and how these will affect the development of the overall business operations.

k) **Sustainability section**. This section captures the structure laid out to ensure that business operations are not only profitable but also sustainable over a long period of time. The planner will have a chance to tell the investor on the type of both internal and external sustainability steps that the business has taken to remain relevant and profitable over time.

l) **Future business projections**. This will deal with the way you want your business to look in the future. This section will also deal with your business visions, goals, objectives and milestones.

m) **<u>Supporting documents</u>** that were used in the developing of the document plan. This the section to list the documents that you used in the preparation of the document. This may be documents such as maps, logistical documents and any other relevant document used in the process. This should also capture other documents that will serve to raise the credibility of your plan document such as product photos, market survey documents and contractual documents if any.

Section 1: Title Page of Business Plan

The title page is the first thing that your investors and funding agencies will look at before actually going into the content of your document. In this way, special attention should be given to this section as it will serve as the first thing that will attract your investors. The title page should include at least the following details;

a) Be sure to include, in the proper area, your business logo. This will serve to give your document an official look and credibility. This will give your document a professional image that will serve to tell your investors that you are not only serious in what you are doing but also committed to professionalism and proper business etiquette. A good business logo should serve to provide a unique touch to your business and tell the investors what you have in terms of business ethics and operations.

b) Business name and a short overview of your document. Here you can explain to potential investors whether the plan is a business plan, a recovery strategy or a business marketing plan. Include a short but precise name that tells the investor the nature of your document in an accurate and short manner. Do not include fancy and unofficial names. Let the name of the document be reflective of the situation without missing the core mission of your process.

c) Enter your name. This should be the name of the entrepreneur or the business owner, manager or any other person that is directly involved in the writing process and intended business operations. In case there are several other business co-owners, include all the names of these individuals if it suits the occasion. There is therefore no need to include too many business names in the title page of your business plan.

d) Write the official titles of the owners or individuals mentioned above. This should be in relation to the business rather than the titles usually put before the names of the persons. For example, you should indicate whether the person mentioned is the owner, the manager or CEO of the business. Remember to include the perfect and the accurate title to avoid any confusion if there happens to be a situation where you need to have an interview with your funding agencies, donors or investors.

e) Enter your business name. This business name should be the official registered business name with the relevant registering authorities. Let the name appear exactly as it appears with the registering authorities. This is because your investors may decide to have a search of your company or business and ascertain its legitimacy.

f) Enter the main address of your business. You can use your home address as your main address in the document if your business is based at home or in a location that does not have a formal business address. If your business has more than one location, it is only wise to include the address of your main office as the main official business address.

g) The title page should also have the contact details of your business such as phone numbers and email addresses. Remember that the numbers used here should be those of the company or business rather than those that are personal. This is important in ensuring that your business assumes a different personality other than that associated with your persona. Let the investors have a number that they can call or communicate with your business and the administration staff there, rather than with you.

h) Include your business number used for identification and taxation purposes. Depending on your territory, country or region, the number may have different names, it is the number used for identification of your business in regard to business tax purposes. Include the number that is used to identify your company if your business is a company.

i) Include the date that your document was prepared. The date should be the one that you finished writing the document not when you started working on the document. This is very important as it can serve as a reference point in the decision on when to do the revision.

j) Include the tables that are relevant to your plan document. These tables may capture such information as tabulated revision history, tabulated communication schedules as well as table of contents. The table of contents should be updated as the plan is being written. It should also be the page that you will get after the title page. This will be the list of the subheading and other relevant document sections alongside their page numbers.

k) The title page should be well printable and professional. Unnecessary details should be omitted and careful steps taken to ensure that the title content does not fall under the second page. The title page should remain one page, and be well written to capture accurate and credible business details. The wording should be legible and straight to the point. Include contact details that the investors can contact you with in a clear and legible manner. Every entrepreneur should be aware that a properly titled business plan is the first step towards attracting investors and serious stakeholders in your business.

l) In this way, the title page should be written in a manner that will give the document a professional and credible business image. Make sure to include all the details without omitting important information. You should be sure to first confirm the details before submitting your business plan to the investors or interested stakeholders. Make sure to include a catchy heading that will tell your investors of your willingness to become an authority in the field that you are venturing in.

m) This is your perfect chance to tell your investors what your business idea looks like and shed light on how you are going to execute this plan from initiation to maturity.

Section 2: Business Details

The business details section is the reason behind formulating, developing and executing any business idea. In this section, you are required to write all what you plan to do as far as your business is concerned. Under the business details section, you are likely to be dealing with the following issues;

a) **<u>Your business purpose</u>**. Here you are to detail the purpose of your business and include the products or services that you trade or intending to trade in. remember to be exhaustive as possible and give accurate information. Briefly outline your main business purpose to give the investor the details of your business products and services. Do not assume that the investor or any other stakeholder will have the information on the products that you sell without outlining the details. If you are selling cars, for example, remember that you need to include the type of vehicles that you deal with for example you can indicate whether these ones secondhand or new or both. The reader will therefore get concrete information that touches on your business type.

b) Include the **<u>details of your business size</u>**. Among the most important aspect here is the number of employees already working with the business or the number of employees your business intends to have. You should also include the annual turnover of your business. If your business is a startup, you should clearly give an estimate of your annual turnover to give the investor information on the business that you intend to operate.

c) **Brief history of your business**. This will capture the period that your business has been in operation. Indicate clearly the achievements that you have had already and what you expect in the near future. If the business is a startup, include the information on how your business will be. Talk about your business plan idea and clear milestones that you need to achieve.

The business details section capture information that is particularly reflective of the nature and formation of your business. This should not only be accurate but also up-to-date. The failure to include the most up-to-date information may result in the failure of your plan in the process of giving your investors a touch with reality on the ground. In this sense, you should make sure that the business details are the most accurate and up-to-date reflection of your business.

Section 3: Business Registration

The business registration section will capture all the official details of your business. Among the most important details that should be inserted in this section include the following;

a) **<u>Enter your business name</u>**. The name inserted here should be the official registered name of your business. If your business is not yet registered, you should write the proposed business name. However, any serious entrepreneur should be aware of the importance of registering your business name. You should have your business name registered by the authorities in your state or country for a proper business aura. Any credible business should have its name registered properly by the relevant authorities. Even before writing your business plan, you should have the business name checked for authenticity and availability. This should be done well in advance to avoid any disappointments in case the business name proposed is not available or has already been registered by someone else.

b) You should then enter the **<u>trading name of your business</u>** in case you want to trade in other names. These names are the ones that you intend or having been trading under. List all the names explaining the purposes of each name. Proper trading names are important in the marketing and advertising circles. You should be sure to use trading names that are uniquely yours by virtual of ownership or copyright. This is important in the sense that they are the ones that will be associated with your business products and services.

c) Indicate the **date that your business was registered**. This is the date that appears in your registration papers. If your business has not yet been registered, you should make effort and registered. This increases the credibility of your plan document and cements the fact that you believe in the business that you do or intending to venture in.

d) Indicate clearly the **areas and locations where your business is registered**. In case that your business has been registered in more than one country or state, you indicate all these areas. If your business has not been registered already, you should be sure of the date and place that you intend to have your business registered. Indicate this and provide more details on why you have not yet registered your business. Note that if the business has not yet been registered, you should have it registered immediately.

e) **Enter the business structure**. This is where you will have to indicate the type of the business that you operate or intending to operate. This section will center on the fact whether your business is sole-proprietorship, trust, partnership, community based, limited or private or a public company where shares will be available for purchase.

f) Depending on your country or state laws, you should provide the **business registration numbers** attached to your business operations. These are numbers that are used for income tax or any other business levies relevant to your area of operation. You should have the dates that the numbers were assigned to your business. If you have not yet acquired these numbers, you should be sure to apply for them as per the rules and regulations governing your particular industry in your country or state.

g) Enter your business **website and domain names**. Nowadays, operating a business without a business website is looked down upon. Any investor will frown upon a company or business that does not have an online presence. If you are serious in your business, find proper and relevant domain names and have them registered for the sole use of your business. Enter these details in this section and be as clear as possible. List all the domain names that your business is intending to use and have them registered for you sole use. A good domain name is the one that matches the name of your registered business names.

h) Enter your **business permits, licenses and other certifications** issued by various authorities depending on your area of operation. Depending with the country, state and regions, different permits and licenses are issued according the operations of the business. There are trade licenses, medical certificates, inspection letters, agent licenses, and a myriad of permits. Be sure to include all of these and make sure you apply for the ones that your business does not already have, ahead of time.

i) This is important because these documents will serve to give the investor the confidence that you are sure of what you are trying to do. In case there is a particular document that is needed but you not yet acquired, indicate this and provide a time-frame that you will have it secured. Giving the necessary documents according to the nature of your business is important in the process of attracting and retaining investors and other valued stakeholders in the industry. showing that you have acquired, or you are in the process of acquiring the necessary permits is way important in raising the levels of confidence in all the persons that you will be interacting with in the process of executing your business plan and business success.

Section 4: Business Premises & Location

It is important to note that the location of your business is as important as the business itself. Proper and credible businesses are known to maintain physical premises where they operate from. However, with the recent technological advancements in the ICT sector, some businesses are operating virtual or hosted offices somewhere away from their geographical operation zones. In this way, this should clearly be indicated and proper reference given. Otherwise, the details of the business premises should be given and a proper map provided as an attachment to the plan document.

Under this business premises section, you are likely to include the following details;

a) **Location of the business**. This is where your business operates from or where you are intending the business will be operating from. A credible business premises is important in winning the hearts of investors as well as winning business and customers. You should indicate clearly the details of the business office space as well as well as the town or city your business is situated in. in this regard, you should be sure to provide the location of your business in relation to popular, known or major landmarks in your area. Just in case you are operating a small retail business for example, you should be sure to give its location in relation to other outlets of the same nature in your area. This section wants you to essentially tell your investors and stakeholders the exact place that your business is located. You can give the street names or floors where applicable.

b) **<u>Rental, Buy and lease details</u>**. These are details that will touch on the business premises in terms of ownership. You should give the details whether the premises are rented or purchased by your business. If you are holding leased premises, you should clearly indicate this and give the details of the lease agreement and duration. This is important in the sense that you may be holding premises that are temporary or tentative. You should also be sure to give lease details that touch on the amount of money that you spend on the rent of the premises. Just in case you have not already acquired business premises, you should clearly indicate this and give an indication of the type of premises, the cost and the location of your desired business premises, or at least the general area.

c) If your business is operating a virtual office, you should give a clear picture of the nature of the office such as the **<u>domain names</u>** as used in the business. Provide the main business website and any other online portals and resources that will serve to give the investors a clear picture of your virtual office arrangement. In this age of advanced technological underlining, you should be accurate enough and detailed to an extent of giving the best that there is. In case of having a hosted or outsourced business office arrangement, you should provide details of these service providers and their locations. For example, if you are using the services of a call center, you should provide the names and the location of the call center or centers. These details should also be captured when writing about the nature of your business and the type of business that you are operating.

d) You may also want o have this clearly outlined in the innovation and uniqueness section, meaning that you do not have to give as much information here. If your business has this outlook, you should be sure to mention and justify this in a section of its own. This is important in the sense that the details will have a clear effect on the business operations and that this should be shown and explained to investors and other stakeholders.

Section 5: Financials

The finance section will deal with all the issues that touch on money that your business will be dealing with or what the finance your business has been dealing with. Among the most important issues that this section should capture include the following;

a) **<u>Creditors table</u>**. This section should present the creditors that are currently dealing with your business. In this way, the table should include the current business creditors in the most detailed manner. You should show the investor the list of your current creditors, the special arrangements put in place to recover the money and any other details that touch on your relations with your current creditors. You should include the name of the creditor, contact details of the creditor, the type of recovery arrangement put in place and the dates for the same. You should also provide the amount due and the date that the money will be recovered. You should show the investor the potential at which your business can do all this if you are just starting up. Otherwise, if you are an existing business entity with many creditors, you should be sure to provide as detailed information as possible.

b) **Debtors table**. Just as you have done with the creditors, you should do the same with your debtors. You should give the investor a clear table of your current debtors, the ones you are in contact with and the ones that you hope to bring on board. You should include the names of your debtors, their contact details, amount expected and the arrangement put in place. Also add the amount that has been agreed upon and the date. If you are just starting up, you should give the projections of your debtors and the arrangement that you have put in place for all this. In the case of an operational business, you should give as much details of your debtors as possible in the most accurate manner.

c) **Government and other stakeholder funding table**. Your investors will need you to show them the table of government, federal, statutory or other stakeholders funding details. List all the funding that you have already applied for and the amount. Give the details of the program, the contacts, and the dates of application and receipt. This sub-section will be dependent on the type of business that you are operating and the possibility whether the business is entitled to such funding from government and other special agencies. Leave this section out if your business operations are not consistent or applicable to these funding sources. Otherwise, give as much detail as possible in case your business is affected.

d) **A Projected cash flow table** should also be included in this section. You should show the investors your expected incoming and outgoing cash that your business is involved in. it is good to note here that this sub-section will list the items of cash that are going out and coming in an emergency or disaster scenario. They should have the dates, the amount and the reasons behind the scenario. This should be a clear indication of the structure put in place to tackle issues that are not foreseeable or those ones that are crisis-dealing in nature. The planner should be focused on the issues that touch on cash flow in cases of disaster or crisis management.

Section 6: Risk Management Issues and Insurance

This is the section that will deal with special structures put in place to cater for the business in terms of risks and insurance needs. Among the most important thing that you need to tell your investors in the business plan include the following;

a) **Insurance sub-section**. This is the sub-section in this stage that will list all the insurance that you have secured for your business and employees. Depending on the type of business that you are operating, the plan document should capture the following;

- *Public liability insurance.* This is the insurance that you have secured that touches on public liability. This will cover the business owner in case of third party death or injury. Remember that this is cover that is very important in your business and will serve to tell your investors that you have the proper structures put in place in case of public liability issues. Indicate the dates and the amounts payable. You should also provide the policy details and the documents attached.

- *Workers compensation insurance.* If your business has employees and depending on the particular statutory requirements, your business should have workers compensation insurance that covers you in case of injury or death on the part of your employees. In many cases, this type of insurance is mandatory for those businesses that have employees, as your business may well have.

- It will serve to show your investors that you are not only serious on the interests of your employees but also that your business is respectful to the laid down statutory requirements in your area that touches on the insurance needs of employees. This a credible plus to the business investment needs. Remember to provide the number of employees that you have, the amount insured and the relevant and important dates of your insurance policy.

- *Product liability insurance.* This is a very important aspect that covers you and your business in case of injury or death occasioned by your business products or services. This will cover your business in case of legal actions taken against your business in effect of your products and services provided. It is important in the sense that your investors will understand the depths that you can go towards making sure that your business is well protected and your products and services are important to the business operations. You should be sure to provide the dates and the amount of your product liability and the policy documents.

- *Professional indemnity insurance details.* These are details of your insurance that covers you in case of legal actions taken against you or the business as a result of your professional advice or actions. It will touch on the insurance that you have put in place to shield the business against legal actions that may be taken due to your professional conduct or actions. Provide the amounts insured, the dates and documents.

- *Business asset insurance*. This is the insurance cover that you have taken for your business assets and premises. It consists of insurance for your motor vehicles, buildings, premises, plants and the like. These insurance covers may be taken against issues such as theft, fire, natural calamities and any other risk for your assets. Provide the details of your business asset insurance, the items insured and the dates. You may also include the policy documents as attachments.

- *Business revenue insurance*. This is the insurance cover that you have taken to protect your business revenue. This covers your business in case of interruptions of any kind or business downturns. It will show investors the level of seriousness that you have gone in terms of having your business operations intact. Provide the amount, the date taken and documentation of the policy if any.

b) **Risk management sub-section**. This should include the risks that your business is likely to encounter and how you plan to deal with the risks. You should list the risks according the likelihood of them happening and the way you need to deal with them. For each risk scenario, indicate the following;

- Describe the risks in detail, and the possible ways that the risk can affect your business. Give details of the scenario and ways it can be reduced, negated or eliminated.

- Give the likelihood that the risk has of occurring. In this way, you should show the investor the chances of this risk happening in the most accurate manner. You will have to tell the investors whether the chances of the risk happening are highly like, likely, unlikely or highly unlikely. The chances should capture the most accurate picture that will also be used by the investors to gauge the viability of your business idea, strategy or commercial proposition.

- Tell the investors the level of impact that the risk is potentially capable of affecting your business. In this way, you should tell the investors whether the impact of the risk to your business is low, medium or high. This is a serious indication that you have done your background research and thought deeply on your business idea and the potential risk impacts of your business idea.

- Show the investors the strategies and structures that you have put in place to prevent these risks, to reduce their impacts, mitigate or take remedial actions. This will the chance to prove to the investor the potential resources and structures at your disposal to manage the risks.

Insurance and risk management section will give you as the business owner of planner a chance to show the investors that you are capable of dealing with those issues that can affect the business in a manner that would have been disastrous if unplanned for. It is a chance for the entrepreneur to show the investors the level of understanding of the risks that the business will be dealing with.

Section 7: Legal Issues and Considerations

In this section, you can provide the investor with issues that touch on the legal side of your business and the relevant legal framework that your business will be operating within. Among the most important legal issues and considerations that should be included in the plan document include the following;

a) The legislation that touches on your business or business operations. In this section, you should list these legislations in terms of the highest impact to your business. This will depend on the type of business that you are or you will be operating. Every industry has legislation that has been developed to either regulate or guide the industry by local and statutory authorities.

Among the most important here are the consumer laws, business laws, export laws and regulations, specific industrial acts and regulations among others. You should be sure to have these legal considerations in place or show the investor the plans that you have to comply with the legislations.

b) Disclosure and general obligations of your business should also be included in this section. This will deal with matters pertaining to your business and tell the investor more on the plans that you have on this area.

One of the very first things that you should be thinking about in making your business plan is the legal essentials that touch on your business. Knowing what legal essentials are relevant to your business industry is the first thing and requirement towards complying. When developing your business plan, you should be sure to show your investors on the level at which you understand the legal situation that will affect your business and the level at which you have or planning to comply. These may touch on leases, contracts, licenses and registrations.

Among the most important of the legal essentials that should be included in this section touch on the following;

c) Provide information on **business registrations**. In every country. All businesses should be registered before actually commencing business. It is a legal requirement that the businesses should be registered as well as honoring copyrights and intellectual property rights applied and respected. The business registration will be important in meeting the tax regulation in every country or state. In this way, you should show the investors that you are compliant in tax issues applicable in your business area or how you plan to become compliant once you start out in case your business is not yet rolled out.

d) **Licenses and permits** are also included in this section. Depending on the type of business that you are operating, different licenses and permits are required. It is your duty to show the investors the level at which you have complied with these requirements by way of listing the licenses and the permits that you have already acquired or planning to acquire. Remember that it is your obligation to research and understand the different types of licenses and permits that your business requires if you do not want to be slapped with fines and other obstacles. Make sure that you have consulted widely on the type of licenses that are required for your business in the local and territorial scenes. Showing the investors the level that you have planned for this is a credible way of increasing the chances of getting that business commitment that you are looking for.

e) Issues touching on **privacy** are also included in this section. It is a legal requirement in many countries and states to have businesses respect the privacy of employees and other individuals directly or indirectly associated with the business. In this way, the investor will want to see the strategies you have put in place on how you will deal with, handle or process personal information in your business relations. The investors may also want to see how you plan to deal with that personal information in terms of direct or indirect marketing purposes.

f) Of importance here also is the plan that your business has in terms of disclosing or sharing personal information with other businesses or partners outside the business or outside the business territory or even overseas if it is applicable in your business. You should be sure to do your research and determine the issues that guide privacy aspects in your area of business. This will tell the investors on how you plan to deal with privacy issues include the details that the investors will share with you in the business operations.

g) Indicate to the investor how you plan to **deal with bullying** in the work place by mentioning the structures and strategies put in place to cater for anti-bullying laws. Bullying refers to when a person or a group of people behave badly, injuriously or unreasonably towards an employee or worker in the workplace. This can be viewed as a risk on the part of the worker's health or safety. The business planner should be able to show the investors on the concrete steps that have been put in place to ensure that this does not happen and if it happens, the remedial actions and structures to be invoked for such behavior.

h) **Issues and structures relating to independent contractors** as opposed to employees. Independent contractors are those persons that are self-employed and provide services to their clients for a negotiated fee. Before you enter into a contract, you will need to determine whether the person is a contractor or an employee. This will guide you on the legal issues that relate to the particular contracts. In this way, you will need to show the investors on the plans that you have laid out for dealing with independent contractors in your business. This will serve to show the investors that you understand this scenario very well and that you differentiate between employees and contractors.

i) **Unfair dismissal**. It is important to understand that there are different laws that touch on the dismissal of employees. Different business sizes have different rules relating to dismissal of employees. Those that have less than 15 employees are usually considered small businesses with different employee dismissal rules. You should be able to show the investors in your plan document on how you plan to deal with employee dismissal in a fair and legal manner. However, this applies to businesses that have employees in the first place and if your business does not have employees, you do not need to include this information.

Section 8: Unique Business Issues or Innovation

In this section, you may list the different research, development and innovation that you are engaged in or you are planning to engage in. this is an important way of telling the investors on what you are planning to do to encourage innovativeness and creativity in your business. Innovation generally refers to the process of creating ingenious and more effective business processes, ideas and products. This is done for the purpose of improving and increasing the success of the business as well as providing more efficient business environment. This does not necessarily mean that you will have to actually engage in inventing or discovering new products, ways or methods of conducting business. Neither does it mean that you will need to invent new business technologies in the process. This rather means that you can change your business models and engage in adaptive actions aimed at improving the success and performance of your business. Among the most important steps to be captured in this section include the following;

a) Provide the plan on how you will **conduct market analysis**, customer needs and wants as well as how you will ensure that your business remains open to new ideas and changes. You will need to provide the investors with the strategy that you will invoke to ensure that your business remains relevant to changing market situations and circumstances.

b) Include a plan how you will **strategically respond** to major business processes that will last through the entire business period.

c) Show the investors the plan that you have in place to **provide leadership** in the areas of innovation. This may touch on the training and development strategies that you have put in place alongside motivational leadership potentials that your business will extend to employees and other stakeholders in the process of doing business.

d) Show the investors the plan that you have put in place to ensure that your business **maintains contact with the relevant stakeholders** in the area of innovation. This will help the investors to understand the plan that you have for product development both internally and externally.

e) You should also include in this section the type of **business consultation** or advise that you plan to use in the innovation process. This will give you the chance to let your investors understand the professional structures that you have put in place for your business innovation needs.

In this section too, you will need to provide details of how you plan to protect your business innovations. Among the most important things that you should include here are the following;

- **Current logos and trademarks**
- Current and potential patents
- **Business designs already registered or those you are planning to register**
- Employee or other stakeholders confidentiality agreements
- **Intellectual property (IP) protection**

- Strategies to ensure that these rights and confidentialities are protected from competitors and other parties.

All these issues should be captured in the business plan in the most accurate and concise manner. This will help the investors to understand the best ways through which the business will deal with innovativeness in the process of development and protection. You will tell the investors the extent to which you understand the fact that innovation is the key to proper competitive advantage for the business.

Section 9: Business Products and Services

This is the section that will serve to give the details of your products or services provided. In this section you can let the investors know the products that your company is dealing with or the products that your business is planning to deal with. Your business plan should capture the following details in the business and services section;

a) Give the ***product details*** of the items that your business is dealing with. List every single product that you are trading in or planning to deal with. The items listed should have proper and accurate product description along with the current price tag of the item. The information given will be used by the investors to gauge the amount of capital that the business operates with and possible financial inputs.

b) Indicate the *market position* of your products. Your investors need to be told where the products fit in the market situation and whether they are high-end or alternatives to existing products offered by competitors. You need to plan for the products in such a way that the document will reflect the market situation in the most accurate manner.

c) Provide the *unique selling point (USP)* by indicating how your products will sell amidst competition or areas where other similar products have failed in the recent past. Here you have the chance to list the advantages or qualities that give your products an edge in the market. This is important in the sense that the investors will have the best opportunity to gauge the success of the products that you are planning to sell. This section will also deal with services that you may need to offer to your customers in order to raise the chances of your business success such after-sales services, transport services among others.

d) *Projected demand* of your products. In this section, you will need to provide the projected demand situation of your product in the period of the next six months and 12 months. You will have to give the projected sales volumes of a single customer in the stated period. This should be in terms of statistical figures consistent with the actual business reality.

e) Include the product or services *pricing strategy* for your business. If your business has a particular strategy, you need to provide and describe this in the most clean and concise manner. You should also provide a clear and accurate justification why you have chosen that strategy among other alternatives. This should be backed with information derived from your market research, projected demands of your products, the expenses incurred among other business issues at hand. This will serve to indicate to your investors and stakeholders the level at which you are at home with your chosen pricing strategy and how it works to give you a business edge in your product market arena.

f) Include the *value* attached to your products and services by your clients and customers. In this sense, you will need to show whether your products are viewed as basic necessities, luxurious products or anywhere in between this. You should be clear enough to reduce chances of erroneous judgment by the investors and other stakeholders. This will also make your thoughts clear on the way you should handle other aspects of the products including packaging, different price points as well as promotions.

g) Indicate your products and services *growth potential*. This is the projected growth and development of your products and services in the near future. You will be guided by looking at your market research statistics, monitoring growth in the industry and doing a proper assessment of the issues that will affect your business positively or negatively. This growth potential should be given in a percentage manner and should be as accurate as possible. This will also serve as a reference point later to see how and to extent your business have met or deviated from the projected business growth.

h) You should also include any *special elements and characteristics* of your products that you believe will bring about success in the future. In this sense, you will be clear on the issues that affect your products in the long run and the ones that will serve to bring forth business success.

Section 10: Business Organization and Ownership

This is the section that will deal with how the business is organized and who are the owners and members of management team. In this section, the following important elements should be captured and included;

a) **An organization chart**. This is a representation of how the business is organized in a graphical or pose manner. This is a visual or graphical representation of the business structure. In the effort of writing and developing a good business plan that can win the hearts of investors in the fastest manner, the plan document should have an attachment that will show the business structure chart. The chart should be filled depending on the seniority of the individuals in the structure representation. The chart should have lines that indicate relationship in the business structure with the senior individuals above the juniors.

b) If your business is a startup or in the recruiting stage, this should clearly be stated by using "vacant" where the names of the individuals are supposed to be. If the whole business structure is "vacant" you need to indicate this by labeling the chart as proposed or tentative chart. In the event that you want to give a prose indication of your organization chart, you can give the names and the positions of individuals with their relationships with each other starting with the most senior members.

c) **Ownership and management sub-section**. In this section, you will have the chance to tell your investors who are the owners and managers of the business. Among the details you need to capture in the plan document includes the following details;

- List of the *names of the owners*. You should include all the owners of the business here and the roles they play in the business. Provide the exact details of each owner of the business in terms of the business activities. Show the responsibilities of each owner in the most accurate manner possible.

- *Management and ownership details*. This will tell the investors who are the managers and the roles played by the owners. If the business is a partnership, you need to list all the partners, their roles and responsibilities in running the business. You will also provide the percentage share of each individual in the most accurate manner. Indicate the special inputs of each person and whether or not there is a contract agreement in place to govern these relationships.

- Business *experience and expertise.* In this section, you should provide the experience and expertise of every owner or partner and why people should invest in this business. You will need to provide the exact years that these individuals have been in this business, the years spent in other business management tasks, previous professional experience, previous and current professional accolades and awards as well as years spent in similar circles. After this is captured in this section, you should be sure to attach copies of professional resumes for every individual listed that will serve as a proof to what the plan document claims.

d) Enter the **details of the major business personnel**. In this section you will give the investors the chance of getting information concerning your business staff or personnel. Among the details to be captured here you need to make sure you include the following;

- The *job title.* This will show the title that each individual is associated with. For example, you can have a job title like the sales and marketing manager, operations manager, sales executive, CEO, CFO, among other job titles.

- *Name of the individual job title holders.* This should be the name used officially in the government recognized documents such as passports or national identity cards.

- *Expected turnover* for each job holder. This should be given in terms of months or years depending on the type of business that you are operating.

- *Experience or/ and skills* of every staff member. This will serve to show the investors the type of brains that you have at your business disposal and the potentials that your business have in terms of success. You include such details as the skill and experience gained in other business operations or the training that the staff member possesses. For example, you can have descriptions such as five years in sales and marketing areas, trained in expert in business communications, etc.

- Remember to attach a copy of *professional resume* for each staff after you have written the plan document as a proof to the claims made. This will give the investors a chance to scrutinize the type of personnel that you have in your business.

e) List the **staff that your business needs** in this section too if the same applies to your case. In the process of listing the vacant positions that you want filled, you will need to indicate the job title, the number of persons that you want in the position, expected staff turnover or the least amount of time that the staff will be required, the skills needed for the vacant position and the date at which the vacant position should be filled.

f) You should also be sure to indicate the method that you will use in the **recruitment process**. You need to indicate whether you will advertise the position online, on the local media or you will recruit existing staff internally or externally as the case may be.

g) In case you do not find the skills that you require in the process of recruiting the necessary staff, you need to include the **training actions** that you will require to ensure that the staff that you have recruited or need to train will undergo. You will be sure to tell your investors whether this training will be done internally, in-house or out-sourced. In order to remain relevant and competitive in business, you will need to show the investors the training that you will offer to yourself, your staff members and any other person in the business period. This will give the investors a chance of knowing how you plan to keep your business and operations skills current and relevant amid changing business and operation circumstances.

h) To ensure that the skills in your staff are maintained and retained you will need to provide a **plan** on how you will undertake this. The plan should capture the way through which particular business responsibilities will be allocated and how the same should remain focused and relevant. This is important in the sense that the owner of the business or the business manager will have a chance to make sure that the business skills are maintained and that they remain relevant for the benefit of the business. You will need to show the investors how the business will make sure that the acquired skills are still useful for the current and ever changing business circumstances in your industry.

Section 11: The Balance Sheet

A good plan must include a current and accurate balance sheet of the business. A balance sheet is a representation of the current state of the business assets and liabilities on a particular date; it works out the exact net asset of the business giving out a clear indication of whether the business is running at a profit or at a loss. It is a very useful tool in the process of working out the business capital and liquidity giving a very clear picture of the health and viability of the business venture.

A good plan should include a balance sheet in the local currency if the plan will be used locally or in dollar if the plan has an international element. This should be for no less than three years term so that it can provide a futuristic angle consistent with the conventional business plan initiatives. You should also be sure to provide the net figures for each as in the total assets and total liabilities.

Among the items that should be included in the balance sheet capture the following;

a) Under *current assets*, you should list the figures for cash, petty cash, pre-paid expenses & inventory.

b) Under *fixed assets*, you should provide the figures for property, land, leasehold, furniture and fittings, computers and other equipment, cars and other machinery, renovations and other improvements and any other fixed asset consistent with your business operations.

c) Under *total assets*, you should provide the sum figure amounts of both current & fixed assets. This will give you the value for your assets.

d) In the section of *current liabilities*, you should include such items amounts the likes of credit card payable, interests and accounts payable, accrued salaries and wages as well as income tax. These expenses and liabilities will depend on the type of business that you are operating and the nature of the payment methods currently in use.

e) In the *long term liabilities*, you should include the loans that you have taken for your business. Include all the loans that your business is counting on.

f) When providing the *net liabilities*, you should give the sum of the current and long term liabilities.

g) The *net assets* will be given by the difference in the total assets and total liabilities. If the figure is negative, then the business is running at a loss and vice versa.

You should be sure to give accurate figures in your balance sheet. Whether you are in business or not, plan document that will attract investors must contain a balance sheet. If you are starting up, you should provide clear estimates and label them as such.

Section 12: Profit and Loss

A good and viable business plan that needs to attract business investors must have a profit and loss section. Profit and loss statement is business tool that deals with business sales and expenses. This is usually developed and recorded in a monthly or yearly basis. This will depend with the type of business as there are some businesses that do this on a quarterly basis. This is a good tool for the development of sales targets and giving the actual profits or loss.

A good and viable business plan document should have a profit and loss statement that covers at least three years. The most important issues captured in the profit and loss statement include the following;

a) Under the *sales section*, you should list the figures for total sales, and the cost of goods sold. The difference of these two less the expenses directly related to the sold item will give you the gross sales of your organization as defined by accounting methods.

b) Under the *expenses section*, you should clearly give the figure amounts of all the expenditure related to the business. These ones, depending on the nature of the business may include office fees, advertising costs, bank fees, interests and other charges, credit card fees, maintenance costs, insurance, stationery, rents, income taxes among a myriad of expenses that are directly related to the business operations.

c) Count the *total expenses* as indicated above and list it as the total expenses.

d) *Net profit* will be provided by the difference in amount in total sales and total expenses.

It is important to note that whether you are already in business or starting up, you will need to provide actual or estimated figures depending on your business juncture. Be as accurate as possible when giving these figures or their estimates.

Section 13: Costing

There is no way you will properly show the amount of money that you need to start up your business without developing and writing a proper costing sheet. In this section, you will list the amount that you have already used or the ones that you plan to spend in the following important areas;

a) *Registration*. This will center on the amount of money spent in the areas of business registration, business names, domain names, licenses and permits, trademarks, logos and vehicles.

b) *Other startup costs* include rents, logistics, internet fees, computer expenses, insurance, raw materials, among many other expenses that you will incur before actually being in business.

c) You will also need to provide *capital and equipment costs* that may include furniture and fittings, motor vehicles, premises, security costs among many other expenses.

d) Once you add up all these costs you will get the **final startup cost**.

It is important to note that the costing is **not limited to startups only**. Even existing and established businesses will have to provide this section in case of business re-adjustments. You must include the estimates of how much your business will cost whether starting up or adjusting to a particular issue. You need to be very particular on this section as it will give your investors the figure that your business venture is looking for in terms of finance. The best way to do this is to be as exhaustive as possible as you may not want to omit some important costs that may affect your business later on when you are starting up with limited resources.

Section 14: Cash flow Statements

For your business plan to attract proper and positive attention from investors, it should have a *cash flow section*. A cash flow statement is an important business tool in the sense that it tracks the movement of cash in and out of your business. It also reveals the trends through which money is moving in and out and can show seasonal cycles when money is moving in and out thereby creating an business in season or payment season. This is important in the sense that the business planner will have the trend and the season when money is needed most for payment and when money is getting in most in order to prepare for it in advance by laying down proper strategies.

In the process of factoring this on your business plan document, you need to give the money that is moving in and the one that is moving out for a period of one year. Among the items that should be captured in the cash flow statement section includes the following;

a) **Opening balance**. This is the amount of money that you have in the bank or at hand in the first month of your cash flow statement. The other month will be the closing balance after the period of 12 months or as per your standard business period.

b) **Incoming cash** section will feature sales, debts collected as well as any other money that is received in the process of business operations.

c) The **total amount** of money that is incoming will be the sum of the opening balance and the money received.

d) Total **outgoing cash flow** will feature the sum of money that is being spent on issues such as business utilities, purchases, fees, insurances, repairs among many other aspects of expenses.

e) The **closing balance** will be given by the total amount of money that has come in plus the opening balance less total amount of money that went out.

It is important to note that you need to provide this statement whether your business is already established or not. In the case of a startup, you will need to provide the most accurate and viable estimates. The more the cash flow statement will be exhaustive, the better the chances that you will capture the reality on the ground and get the funding that will be consistent with your business needs.

Section 15: Break Even Analysis

In order for your plan document to be credible and appealing to the investors, you also need to provide an analysis of your business break even. This analysis refers to the point at which your business balance is zero. This is when the business income and the business expenses are the same. This is when your income covers your expenses in the exact manner. In the process of providing this analysis, you will need to have a time frame, the average cost of every product and the fixed cost of the time frame selected.

Once you have these details in terms of figures, you should consider the following in your break-even analysis;

a) Calculate price percentage that is the **profit**. This can be done by subtracting the product cost from the average price of the product. After you have done that, you divide the results by the average price of the product in question.

b) Determine your break-even point, the number of product units sold that is needed to **break even**. Divide the fixed costs of the product for the period chosen by the average price of the product less the average cost of each product.

c) To determine the **total sales** to break even, you will need to multiply the number of units sold by the average price of each product sold.

This analysis is important in the sense that it will give the investors a chance to have a deep insight into your business affairs. Even when your business is not yet operational, you need to ensure that you have given proper and accurate estimates of your break even analysis.

Great Business Plan Writing Tips

Before and after writing your business plan, you need to bear in minds that for proper writing procedure, implementation and execution of your plan, need proper thoughts. Among the most important writing tips for your plan document include the following;

a) Do thorough and proper business *research*. Knowing what you need and how to utilize what you have will give you an edge in your plan writing procedure. You will be able to provide proper forecasts and estimates. This will serve to develop a document that will suit your needs and attract investors in sufficient great numbers.

b) Be clear on *who the plan is being written for*. In this way you need to determine whether the plan is being written for use internally or it will be used to seek funds and investors alike. This will give you an edge on what you need to include, the length and the tone of the document. A good plan document for your investors needs to be exhaustive and comprehensive as possible while maintaining an official tone throughout the writing process.

c) There is no need to try to finish your document in one go. You do not have to deal with or factor in all the sections as some may not apply in your business case. You should write the sections that will touch on your business situation and leave out those ones that do not apply. In the event that you feel you do not have enough information on a particular section or issue, it is important to look for more information or seek consultations from our business partners or business professionals. There are professionals available who can help you in the sections that you feel you are not confident enough.

d) Make sure that you have indicated whether the figures that you are using are estimates or actual figures. When you are starting up, you should give figures that are accurately representative of the situation at hand. Make sure to let your investors know that the figures that you are giving are estimates and that they are justifiably consistent with your plan.

e) Remember to write the business summary last. Remember to put it first in the plan document. In this section, use as few words as you can; but make sure that these words capture the gist of the plan. Here you want your investors to quickly get what you want to communicate and still get motivated and interested in your plan.

f) Just like any other written work, you need to do a thorough proofing of your document. The best way to do this is to let the document cool off a little by giving yourself some time to rest after writing it. After a little rest, you can now proof read your document to remove the errors that may tarnish the professional look of your business plan. The other way is to get impartial yet informed persons to proof read your work. This is important in the sense that errors, omissions, mistakes and other negative elements in the plan will serve to deter your investors from getting the motivation your business would otherwise elicit.

g) When you have finished your business plan, do not stick it off the table. Perform constant review of your document to make it relevant and up-to-date. A good document should be reviewed regularly in order that it remains relevant and useful.

h) Share the document once you have completed with the people that matter in your business. Let your investors have the first look in the event that you need to get them on board. Do not let you competitors have a look at your document as this may give them an advantage.

i) Protect not only the document but also the content of your business plan. You may want to sign confidentiality contracts as well as registering for intellectual property and patents to some of the ideas that you may include in the innovation section.

Business Plan Summary

The summary section is one of the most important sections of your business plan. This section briefly summarizes the contents of your business plan in not more than a page. It will touch on all sections in a brief but concise manner. It will be written last but should appear first in your plan document. This is because it serves as a summary of the aspects of the whole document and an overview of what you want your investors to know. Among the areas that should be included in the summary captures the following;

a) Under the business details, you need to include the following parameters;

- **Enter the business name as registered or the proposed name if the business has not been registered.**

- Include the business structure of the business such as sole proprietorship, partnership, company and the like.

- **Enter the numbers that are associated with your business such as those for tax purposes.**

- Enter the business location, if you have more than one operational base; enter the one that is the main office.

- **Enter the business start date. This is the date on which you started operating or when you opened an office.**

- Provide the list of the owners of the business.

- **Describe your expertise in a brief sentence.**

- Provide the list of services or products that you are selling or planning to sell. Include an anticipated demand situation for your products.

b) You should have a business future section in the summary. Here you should have the following;

- You should give your **vision and mission statement**. In order to do this perfectly and briefly, you should use bullet points.

- **Goals and objectives** should clearly be outlined for your business. This should be both your long term and short term goals.

c) In the market segment of the summary section, you should ensure that you have captured the following;

- Provide your **target market** and why you think they will prefer your products rather than go to your competitors.

- Include a brief **analysis of your business strategy**; how you will go the market, how you will attract and maintain customers and why you think the strategy will work.

d) Under the financial section of the summary, you need to factor in these details below;

- *Sales estimates* and forecasts should be provided here.

- Include the analysis of your *profit estimates*.

- Let the investors know how much money that you will require *initially and up-front.*

- *Where* will you get these funds, how much are you willing to meet on your own and how much do you want to source from other sources?

Remember that the content that you will have in the summary section should be reflected in details in the other sections of your plan document. The summary will serve only to give a quick overview of the business plan.

Conclusion

A business plan is a document that captures all the intended business activities, actions and future. It provides a guide to the business owner or operator towards business success. This is roadmap that the business owner will follow to ensure that business activities are planned before hand and executed according to fore-laid stipulations.

Many small business owners do not see the reasons why they should have a written business plan claiming that the document is only for big multinationals. Other large businesses argue that a business plan is only for those firms that are just starting up or suffering from losses or lost business. The truth is that any business whether large or small, whether starting up or strongly established should have a clear and credible business plan. This will help the businesses to thrive amidst stiff competition.

A well drafted, crafted, concise and credibly written business plan is a very important document not only in business operations but also in the process of looking for funds and investors. A winning business is the one will the most concise and credible plan. There is no way you can source for business funds without giving a proper plan of how you want your business to look. The plan should be futuristic in character and capture all the business elements in the most logical and truthful manner.

The best thing about a credible business plan is the fact that it provides a business with a reference position for the manager or owner to return to in the course of business operations. The pleasure of looking at your plan and seeing how far you have come in business operations is greatly motivating. It will help you to gauge whether you are on track or whether you have drifted from your original goals and objectives. The document will help you as a business owner to think deeper and more analytically when it comes to your business area. The act of putting ideas and concepts concerning your business on paper is important while getting all the information concerning your competitors provides an edge in business operations.

When writing a business plan, you should be clear in your minds about what your business is all about. Include all the details about your business and come up with a catchy title if you want to win the hearts of the investors. In addition to this, the plan should give clear indicators of your business finance in the finance section. Other sections that a business plan should have include the summary section (which should be short and precise and filled last), details section, legal section, sustainability plan section, operations section, balance sheet, cash flow, profit and loss statement, costing section, business ownership section and conclusion depending on the type of business in question. Different business types will have different sections while startups may not have certain sections like profit and loss statement.

The plan should capture as much details as possible and should be accurate and concise. Writing a business plan that will be of interest to investors is usually a time-consuming exercise. However, the good that comes with a credible plan way much outweigh the time spent drafting this important document.